Aikido: My Path of Self-Discovery

Kim Barton

Published by Dala Press

Photo Credits

Front cover: Joe Buglewicz

Author Photo: Akiko Yamamoto

All O'Sensei quotes taken from The Art of Peace by Morihei
Ueshiba, Translated by John Stevens

ISBN: 1-950667-00-6
ISBN-13: 978-1-950667-00-0

DEDICATION

To Judith Robinson Sensei, 6th dan.
For being my teacher. For always encouraging me. For bringing
aikido into my life.

CONTENTS

FORWARD BY HANS GOTO, SHIHAN

It seems to me that in the study of Aikido, we are all guides and we are all travelers on the Way or Path. The question I have asked myself over the years is "Where is this Path leading me?" Is this Path a matter of becoming a master of skills? Is it a striving to become an enlightened being? Or is it to become the best human being that one can be?

I believe that Kim Barton has taken on this personal exploration with wit, emotion and quite a bit of charm to share her Aikido path. She has mixed blog writing with poetry, story-telling as well as personal insights in a delightful 'buffet' describing her journey in Aikido.

If you have practiced Aikido or any discipline for a few years, you might recognize her discoveries, stumbling blocks, and her gratitude and joy for all of her like-minded 'travelers' who have encouraged and supported her over the years. It is a personal yet universal journey and tale.

I am certain that you find your own discoveries and resonance in this book. I know that I have.

Hans Goto
San Anselmo, California

INTRODUCTION

I began training in aikido fifteen years ago, and it would be impossible to relate how much it has changed my life. The way I see the world, and the way I travel through the world physically, emotionally, and spiritually, has been profoundly altered by my aikido practice. As the essays in this book will show, I've thought a lot about aikido— in the universal sense and also in terms of my own practice.

I still have moments in class or especially during a seminar when there are a lot of people on the mat when I look around and wonder how I got there. I had never in my entire life once thought of practicing a martial art; honestly, it was not on my radar of sports to take up or hobbies to pursue. Not even a little bit! The way I found aikido is described in the essay *My Aikido Path*.

I'm fortunate I found a wonderful dojo where I could train, where my teacher knew how to nurture my aiki spirit, and where I found a community of aikido friends. Many of the people who trained at the dojo when I started are no longer there; they've moved to other cities or states, or have simply moved on. It happens. Lives change. Priorities switch. A few of them were my mentors, and I still miss them even though they've been gone for a long time. Their names still get mentioned when I'm training or teaching, and their legacy remains in me. New people have come up the ranks, and they are now my aikido family. I'm grateful to have trained with every single person who has stepped through our doors. Through it all, my teacher has been consistent. She is dedicated to her students, and she constantly pushes me to be better.

The essays in this book are not in any specific order. I tried to clump essays together that seemed to fit, or, if a theme appeared, then I put those together. In some of the essays, I explain terms and other aspects of aikido that will be common knowledge for aikido practitioners, but unfamiliar to non-aikido readers. I've done this for the benefit of those readers who might not know anything about aikido, or, at least, are unfamiliar with some of the terms.

For the most part, the only thread that connects all of these pieces is they are all my own insights into aikido. In some, I was inspired by a quote from O'Sensei or Bruce Lee; in others, the impetus was something that came up in practice or inspired by a teacher.

Unless specifically mentioned, like the quotes from O'Sensei or teachings from a visiting teacher, all the revelations and discoveries written down in this book came from my regular practice under the tutelage of my teacher, Judith Robinson. It is under her guidance that I've had the opportunity and safety to explore my aikido training. Because she created a dojo in which she encouraged us to think about our aikido, I was able to explore my practice deeply. She also encouraged us to step outside of her training, so I attended seminars taught by other teachers both within and outside of my dojo's lineage.

Of course, none of this would have been possible if not for Morihei Ueshiba, O'Sensei. Everything I do on the mat and everything I write originates with this incredible art he created. Although O'Sensei is no longer with us, his art lives on in all aikido practitioners all over the world. There are different "styles" of aikido, but we all do "aikido." We all follow O'Sensei's teachings in our own way.

I'm grateful to him for creating this art. It has transformed my life, and I know it's transformed the lives of many others

"Everyone has a spirit that can be refined, a body that can be trained in some manner, a suitable path to follow. You are here to realize your inner divinity and manifest your innate enlightenment."

~Morihei Ueshiba (O'Sensei)

BUDO

Soft hands cradling my head,

Spinning in a spiral

Bottom to top

Flung out

Gasping.

The tears flow then,

Purging.

No longer afraid of the dark

Terrified of the light,

Embracing it.

Exposed and enveloped,

Cradled in the soft rush of

Flowing skirts.

Tempered by the harsh smack of

Hardened sticks.

Embraced by the love of

Budo

~2007

WHAT IS AIKIDO?

A ikido is often called the Art of Nonresistance or The Non-Fighting Art, because the founder, Morihei Ueshiba, believed that the ultimate goal of Aikido is not the defeat of others, but the defeat of the negative habits in one's own mind. As O'Sensei (Great Teacher or Master), said:

"True victory is victory over oneself."

The word Aikido itself speaks of its peaceful nature.

Ai means "harmony" or "joining together."

Ki means "life force."

Do means "the way."

A definition of Aikido, then, might read as "the way to harmonize life force."

As O'Sensei said,

"The Art of Peace begins with you. Work on yourself and your appointed task in the Art of Peace. Everyone has a spirit that can be refined, a body that can be trained in some manner, a suitable path to follow. You are here for no other purpose than to realize your inner divinity and manifest your innate enlightenment. Foster peace in your own life and then apply the Art to all that you encounter."

These are words I think we could all use to follow, no matter what path we choose to travel down.

THE PRACTICE OF PEACE

*"The **choice between love and fear** is made every moment in our hearts and minds. That is where the peace process begins. Without peace within, peace in the world is an empty wish."* -Paul Ferrini (bold added)

This quote is so very aikido. The "choice" between love and fear—that is what aikido is all about, especially if you think of fear as arising out of hate or anger. Every moment in aikido is about choice—will I choose to diffuse the conflict with aiki, or will I react with violence? According to O'Sensei, choosing peace (aiki) is choosing the path that is in harmony with the universe. When someone attacks us (and this can be physical or verbal or emotional) that person is out of sync with the universe; he or she is off balance. How then, are we going to deal with this person? With peace or with violence? If we are in balance and in harmony with the universe, then we should be able to act with peace and diffuse the conflict without violence. If we are not in balance with the universe, at peace "within," then it can be difficult for us to react peacefully. We meet the conflict with our own conflicted heart and mind. The conflict then escalates.

This is why peace has to come from within. This is why I practice aikido.

Through aikido, I put myself in stressful situations where someone "attacks" me. I have to learn to deal with this conflict in an aiki way, in a peaceful way. It's one thing to talk about being "peaceful" and that we should love everyone. It's quite another to live it when someone is trying to hit you over the head with a heavy wooden sword! Although our practices are done in a safe environment, often our bodies are tricked into believing the danger is real and reacting that way. I've been on the mat knowing my partners are not trying to kill me or harm me, and yet every part of my body screams to either run away or take this person out.

I must practice the peaceful solution. I can't simply talk about it. I'm working to train myself to remain calm and react with a peaceful heart, a heart that wants to handle the situation with the least amount of harm to everyone involved.

It can be a difficult road to follow. There are days when what I'd really like to do is hit someone. And the thing is, I would never have known that, some days, I react to aggression with thoughts of violence if I had never stepped onto an aikido mat. The mat is a training ground to learn about our tendencies and to overcome them. The practice of peace starts with me, and it is on the aikido mat where I begin that practice.

~2013

MY AIKIDO PATH

I wrote this in 2007 when I was up for promotion to shodan (first-degree black belt). My teacher asks all of us who test for dan rank to write an essay on how aikido affects our lives. This was my story.

Martial arts had never been an activity I ever gave any thought. Not once did I think I should take up a martial art as a sport. However, once I started reading and studying Eastern religions and philosophy, I started seeing references to aikido. It was said to be the most spiritual of the martial arts. Aikido kept popping up in my reading, but I put the idea aside for the time being; after all, it was a martial art and not really for me. I filed the information away.

One night I had a dream. I was in a dark and futuristic looking warehouse, and I was in danger. In fact, bad guys pursued me and tried to kill me! I ran and fought and was absolutely amazing in my dream, fighting in a beautiful and powerful style. I could move my body in ways I never thought possible. To be honest, the dream may have been initially brought on by watching the movie, *The Matrix*, but the fighting was not entirely like it was in the movie. It was not impossible. I did not dodge bullets. I did not run up walls. I did not fly. I did, however, flip myself around, twirling, and spiraling. This fighting dream became a serial dream. Night after night, week after week I had it—always the same. In danger, I fought in a remarkable way, twisting and turning and flipping, and always getting away. I woke up tired and worn out. At first, I found the dreams thrilling, but after a while, I grew tired of them.

Months later I read George Leonard's book, *The Way of Aikido*. As I read about his aikido experience I had an insight. This was the fighting of my dreams! I'm supposed to do this! A few months later I decided to do it. I looked up aikido to find dojos in my town. There were four. I called the dojo with "traditional" in the name, because I instinctively knew that was the type of martial art I wanted. I called the number and I talked to Robinson Sensei, and I was pleased to discover the teacher was a woman. Everything about what Robinson Sensei said sounded inviting. I never called another dojo. I never visited another dojo. I went to the dojo to watch a class and was amazed at how happy everyone seemed. This was a martial art and everyone was smiling! Afterward, students came up to me to ask what I thought. To be honest, I thought it looked weird. They understood. I came back for my first class and it felt weird too. I remember thinking during tai no henko that this wasn't the fighting in my dream. Maybe I had made a mistake.

I took a few classes and then had to stop for a while due to family issues. A couple of months later I went back. Maybe I shouldn't do this, I thought, maybe this isn't the right time. But something inside me pushed me on—a voice in my head telling me to continue. I went to the dojo, and when I walked in the door people remembered me. One student even jumped up and down and was happy to see me come back! From that moment on I never looked back, never had any regrets about my decision, and never strayed from my aikido path. There were times when I stumbled and wondered if I could do it, if I wasn't too small and weak and delicate to be a martial artist. There were times when I was so frustrated that I cried. However, the thought of stopping, of not doing aikido anymore, never surfaced. Quitting was never an option. My path was laid before me, and it seemed that nothing would stop it.

I had a lot of help along the way of course. Would I have continued if it hadn't been for Robinson Sensei, and for my sempai? Would I have even joined if it hadn't been for the people in the dojo? Because, as I look back it seems to me that the students and teachers of the dojo are what kept me going. I was incredibly lucky to have so many remarkable aikido people surrounding me. There was a strong sense of fellowship at the dojo. I had so much help and guidance and care.

I also knew, intellectually, that aikido was my individual journey to take. Somehow, though, I didn't allow myself to take the journey in my own way. I allowed my sempai to cloud my vision and block my path. Around the time I became second kyu, I had a vision. I was in my gi and hakama walking along a path (my aikido path). In front of me on this path stood all my sempai. They blocked my way. I realized for the first time that I couldn't get through because I was blocked. There was no malicious intent in the blockage, no desire to hold me back, no ego—just...in the way. As I stopped to take this all in a giant hand (mine, I suppose) came down and pushed everyone out of the way and onto the edges. Now the path was clear.

My sempai were still with me, but now they milled around on either side of my path. In fact, my need to walk this journey alone was so pronounced that all the sempai walked on the opposite side of a fence from me. I could see them, touch them, talk to them, and yet I remained alone. The most striking image of this vision was that the path I traveled on became huge with the blockage gone. My path was clear, open, and wide. I felt like a whole new leg of the journey was upon me. Now my way was truly my way. I felt lighter, less burdened, and carried fewer expectations. I realized I had to do aikido my way; a way in sync with my body, my personality, my ki.

For many months I continued on that wide open path, continuing on my aikido journey within my own personal space. I felt like I'd grown as an aikido practitioner. The seed had been planted; my teacher and sempai watered and cared for me, but this was a time for me to actually grow. Occasionally, I fell back and relied on my sempai too much. I relied on their being in class, working with me, giving me their invaluable advice and friendship. I started to feel blocked again—too reliant on others. This time, though, I knew my trap. This was to be one of my obstacles. As I relied heavily on my parents and siblings growing up in my family, so too did I lean on my aikido "family." I became aware of my need and overcame it.

Recently I had another vision. I was on my path again, the same one as before, only this time, not as wide. I was able to walk closer to my sempai, include them more intimately again on my journey. The fence was gone, and they walked beside me, not in front of me as before. As I looked up the path I could see a mountain. In my previous vision, I could see nothing ahead of me. Perhaps significantly, the mountain looked like Mt. Fuji. I could only see the base of the mountain, not the peak. The peak was not blocked from view by clouds or any other impediments—it simply wasn't in my sights. Sensei has mentioned that when you pass your shodan test you are at the base of the mountain. All the work and testing up until that point is your process of getting to the mountain.

The length of time to my shodan test is now measured in weeks, not years. The base of the mountain is in view. Perhaps when I get to the base I'll be able to get a glimpse of the summit, or maybe I'll just be able to see the next plateau. Perhaps the summit will never be in view. One thing I'll know is whatever happens, whatever the view of the mountain, and whoever may be walking with me, I always followed my path.

~2007

THE CIRCLE AND THE SPIRAL

I wrote this early in my aikido training.

I often think of aikido in philosophical terms. When a teacher gives advice about how to do a technique physically, I sometimes translate it into advice on how to live my life. It doesn't always happen, and I'm not always sitting in class listening to my sensei thinking, "hmm, now how could that apply to my life?" There are times, though, when it hits me like a slap in the face. I can feel it physically, and it seems as though I've discovered something wonderful.

One day while sitting in meditation, an insight from aikido hit me. It was the concept of moving my uke (the person attacking me) in a spiral motion rather than a circle. When I do ura (a turning movement) or any kind of turning technique where I take uke from a high spot to a spot on the ground, ideally I turn her in a spiral rather than a circle. If I turn uke in a circle...nothing happens. She can go round and round and I'll never take her down, and I never fully take control of her balance. When I have trouble with ikkyo ura, I am probably moving in a circle rather than a spiral. If I move uke in a spiral, from the high point where we both meet to the low spot on the mat, then it works, and I should have control of uke's balance throughout the entire technique.

It occurred to me that this concept of the circle and the

spiral applies to how I deal with life problems, especially those problems that keep coming back to me time after time. I realized that I'm dealing with these recurring problems as circles rather than spirals. First, it's a circle because the problem comes back to me again and again. The reason it comes back is that I always deal with it on the same level. I handle it in almost exactly the same way every time it surfaces. I think about it the same, and I try to solve it in the same way. This never works!

If I deal with these problems as spirals they'll work themselves out. Instead of thinking about them and acting on them in the same way as I have in the past, I need to deal with them on a different level and on a different plane. It's the spiral. Each time I encounter the problem, I need to deal with it on a different level of engagement. In this way, it will eventually be solved.

That's how the spiral works differently and better than the circle. When I'm in the circle mode (in aikido or in life) I always come back to the same place. My uke and my problem are in the same place. The balance of my uke isn't broken, and my problem isn't altered. In the spiral, the plane of existence breaks. I don't come back to the same place; I keep moving down towards the end. The balance of my uke breaks a little bit every time the plane moves, and my problem cracks every time I move downward.

The way for me to do this is to focus on the end rather than on the problem. If I've got all of my attention on uke during ikkyo ura, then I'll instinctively move in a circle. I cannot move towards the conclusion if I'm concentrating on my partner. I must focus on the end—on where I want her to be rather than where she is. I put my focus on the spot on the ground where I want my partner to end up. This also allows me to open my awareness to my surroundings, so I know if something else is coming to sideswipe me.

This all corresponds to life problems as well. If I focus on the end result, and where I want to be rather than focusing on the problem as it is now, then I can get to that end and break the cycle. I also need to open my awareness to my surroundings in daily life too. Only in this way can I be open to new and more creative solutions to my problems.

~2005

THE FOURTH WAY

Fight, Flight, or Freeze. The three ways humans deal with an attack or an extremely stressful situation.

Aikido training offers a fourth way—Blend. Absorb an attacker's energy. Redirect it. Change the nature of the conflict.

The way to do this is to maintain your own posture, your own strength, your own space. Relax. Not in a loosey-goosey kind of relaxation where your muscles are useless, but rather an engaged ready-for-anything relaxation. Like a cat ready to pounce. When an attack comes, accept it and change it from conflict to something more harmonious.

Over the years, I've heard this from several aikido teachers. What we are doing in our aikido training is to teach our bodies to override the animal instincts of fight, flight, or freeze and move instead to the more discerning part of our brain—the part that can offer another solution to conflict.

This is so hard to do! When an attack comes in, even if it's in the safe place of the dojo, with partners I know and trust, the animal reaction kicks in. When a big guy twice my size comes barreling in at me with a heavy wooden sword aimed at my head, or even to grab my arm, my first reaction is to back away. My body screams: Flight! If he latches on, then I want to Fight. It takes a lot of work to switch gears, to concentrate on my own form and to realize that if I maintain my own "space" then I can work with the attack and not fight against it.

When this works, when the discerning part of the brain kicks in and performs aiki, or "joining together," it is a nice feeling for everyone. Those of us in the dojo know it has worked when we get up from the mat with smiles on our faces.

It's nice to know there is another choice. Fight, Flight, Freeze. BLEND.

~2016

"THE EASY WAY IS ALSO THE RIGHT WAY"

"To me, the extraordinary aspect of martial arts lies in its simplicity. The easy way is also the right way, and martial arts is nothing at all special; the closer to the true way of martial arts, the less wastage of expression there is...It is not daily increase but daily decrease; hack away the unessential."
~Bruce Lee.

This is one of my favorite quotes. "Hack away the unessential." I think this can be meaningful in all aspects of life, not just the martial arts. We all have clutter and junk in our lives—useless physical objects lying around the house, unfinished projects, and even relationships that no longer work. When I feel like I need to de-clutter my life, I go to the physical things—the excess junk. Often what I really need is to cut away activities in my life that are no longer useful or to finish projects that have been hanging over my head for a long time.

On the aikido mat, though, simplicity is especially meaningful.

Aikido is difficult and complicated. I've been training for almost nine years, and I still feel like a beginner. I feel like I could practice for the rest of my life and not even come close to understanding what it's all about. What can make it even more difficult is my unconscious insistence on making it even harder than it needs to be.

"The easy way is the right way." Always, always, always.

There are days when I insist on trying to fight my way through a technique. Aikido is all about NOT fighting. In aikido, you are supposed to use your opponent's strength against him. If done properly, the person attacking you should essentially throw himself. If done properly. When I'm making my aikido more difficult, I try to use strength (ha!) and muscle my partner into the position I want him. I pull and push and maneuver him.

This is not the easy way. Nor is it the right way.

I often work with men twice my weight and sometimes a foot taller than me. The right way is to allow all of their height and weight to come to me, get unbalanced by me getting out of the way or turning, and then watch as he flies through the air or falls to the ground. That is also the easy way. It certainly sounds easy. It IS easy when I get out of my own way and allow it to happen...when I don't try to complicate things by FORCING it to happen.

When I try to force things to happen, I am being wasteful, "wastage of expression." I waste my energy, and I waste my natural strengths by not using them to their full potential. My smallness can be an advantage. A big guy has to strike down at me, and it's to my advantage because he could be thrown off balance by trying to lower himself to my height. A big guy also has the disadvantage of momentum—once he gets going, all I have to do is get out of the way, break his balance (kuzushi) and then his size will do all the work to keep him going forward and down. It's hard for him to stop his momentum and regroup to try another attack. By that time, I'm out of the way and ready for what's next, or else I've gotten away to safety.

I know when my aikido works, because it is easy and simple. Afterward, I even marvel at how easy it was! There are times when I finish a technique, throw the person, and think "that was easy."

Easy, simple...right. The "daily decrease" is truly the way of the martial artist.   ~2013

THE 'SHO' IN SHODAN

I recently hung the certificates I received for earning my first and second level black belts. They are beautiful certificates, filled with Japanese kanji, and look like artwork.

As I hung them, I wondered why the first level black belt is referred to as sho and not ichi since ichi is the number one in Japanese. All the other ranks are done by number: ni, san, yon, and so on. What is special about the first one?

I discovered that one meaning for sho is "first," which makes sense.

But another meaning is "beginner." This says so much to me, because that is how I felt when I earned my first rank—like a beginner. The test itself was like a birthing process, a coming-of-age. It was difficult. I broke down on the mat. I was pushed to my limit both physically and emotionally.

When I completed the testing and earned my belt and new rank, I felt like I was just starting on my journey as an aikido practitioner. I felt like my aikido journey up to that point had been a walk on a level path. It had peaks and valleys, of course, but I could see where I was going.

As a new black belt, I had a vision that I was standing at the base of a mountain looking up. I'd made it that far, but the hard part had begun. I had to climb the mountain.

Thinking of this as a beginning rank also reminded me of all I don't know. The more I travel on my aikido path, the more I discover all I have yet to discover.

Attaining a black belt was by no means an attainment of an ultimate goal. It was the beginning of a new path.

~2014.

JOURNAL ENTRIES

While collecting my blog posts and essays for this collection, I also came across entries into my journal. I started an aikido journal when I began my training and stopped writing in it when I became a shodan. These entries show how transformative testing for my first black belt test was. I'm including them as they were written, with only the names of a few people removed.

I have been on such an emotional roller coaster with the process of testing for my black belt. First, I was having trouble even being able to do aikido properly! Then I started feeling really emotional. I was up and down, I'd tear up at the slightest provocation, and I'd have days where I'd lash out at ----.

One day at aikido we were all sitting in a circle after advanced class and sensei told me to breathe. I told her I felt like I was becoming invisible. She said I was gathering up "ki" and I needed to release it. She then said to all my sempai that I either needed group hugs or for them to tell me to get a grip. Someone gave me a hug and I almost broke down, then I put my head on [sempai's] shoulder and cried because I was asked what I needed to work on. I just wanted to go away. I told a couple of the guys on two separate occasions that this emotional roller coaster felt like I did when I was pregnant. [Sempai] told me it was an apt metaphor because I was filling up with aikido. [A different sempai] told me that dan tests are like giving birth to yourself.

Now I'm stressed out because I am the center of attention every time I go to class. We have special classes for us to prepare for our dan tests and I have to get up and perform. Sensei has me as her uke a lot when she's demonstrating techniques for the class. I have to be an uke whenever one of the brown belts is testing. I have to practice my randori in front of the class every time I go to a night class. It's getting hard for me to go to class. I don't like being the center of attention. I like to be under the radar!

When [sempai] and I practice our weapons demo I have to put so much intensity and energy into it that I'm totally spent emotionally afterward. I took a bad break fall today and almost starting crying and told him that I'm too "weak and delicate" to do this.

I'm feeling spent but I know this is where I'm supposed to be. This feeling of utter exhaustion both physically and emotionally is where you learn the most. Your brain shuts down and you can learn so much. I've felt like this before during seminars. It doesn't make it any easier.

Sensei told me that I'll get to a place where I don't want to go to class anymore, but she said the only way to overcome that is to go to class and train! I know she's right. Luckily, my actual physical aikido is going well. I feel great when I'm actually doing it. It's all the spaces in between that are hard.

I'm being mindful of the whole experience. It's turning out to be quite a ride! I'm surprised by the emotional difficulty I'm having with this. I thought my test would be no big deal. I guess I was wrong!!

So, I finally broke down and cried in aikido, on the mat, while a bunch of people were training. I've avoided doing this for 3 years—I've cried right outside the dojo, in the dressing room, and in my car, but never on the mat!

I had to get up in front of everyone and teach weapons with [sempai] today. For some reason it was completely overwhelming for me. I had to work hard to keep it together while I was in class. Then during open mat I felt so undone that I went in the dressing room, hoping to be able to cry. I sat on the floor and curled up but couldn't cry, and not for lack of trying.

Then I went out onto the mat and tried to train with beginners because I thought they'd be safe. But, sensei came up to me and said, "Why don't you work on your shodan test?" So, she starts talking to me about stuff on my test and I'm feeling shaky. She then tells me about a woman who was all blocked up in her first chakra before her shodan test. I tell sensei that it's in my solar plexus. I tell her it's so bad that I'm having trouble breathing. I start to tear up. She mentions that some people have to lie on pillows to help with that. I tell her I have to lie on my stomach with my fist on my solar plexus and as I tell her I push on it. Bam! All of a sudden it all came out. I sank to the floor, put my head on my knees and started sobbing. She sat next to me, rubbed my back, and talked to me about this whole journey.

I looked up at one point to see [sempai] and [sempai] standing there near me watching me—we were supposed to be working together. For some reason, I didn't care. Anyway, I finally pulled myself together and then sensei tells us what she wants us to work on. It was great. It was like, you've had your cry, now back to training. [Sempai] and [sempai] never mentioned it. We actually had a great time and were laughing much of the time we trained!

The cry was like so many cries I've had in aikido. It feels good. After I'm done I feel all clean and new like when we've had a cool rain on a hot day. It's a relief. After class [sempai] comes up, gives me a hug and we have a nice talk about how we feel. I feel so blessed that I'm being nurtured by these people. I sometimes can't believe how kind and loving they all are. I love them very much. They've become a family to me.

~2007

THE RIGHT SONG

☯

I listen to music all the time. When I write, cook, clean, and drive. There are times when a particular song or group of songs attaches to what I'm doing at a moment in time. I have songs that relate to certain characters in my fiction writing. In this case, there were particular songs that suited my aikido mood when I prepared for black belt tests. I wrote this thinking about how songs fit my mood during testing.

Every time I tested for a dan rank, I listened to one particular song or one particular band when I drove to the dojo. This went on for the three months or so that I prepared for my test. I'm not sure why this happened, why one song would hit me so hard as I trained for a test.

When I prepared for my shodan (first degree) test, I listened to Depeche Mode. I listened to one song in particular—*Halo*. Preparing for that test was one of the most taxing times of my life. I was stressed and freaked out about the whole process. When I think about the lyrics to Halo, it makes sense as to why I played this particular song so much:

"I can feel/ the discomfort in your seat/ and in your head it's worse," and *"when our worlds/ they fall apart/ when the walls come tumbling in."*

For my nidan test, I listened to Earth, Wind and Fire

(EWF). Strange to go from Depeche Mode to EWF, but there it is. Like I said, I can't explain it. The only thing I do know was that I was exceptionally calm all during the preparation for the test, so calm my fellow dojo mates kept trying to push me into getting stressed out or keyed up. They'd do things like tell me I was testing that day when I walked in the door. Nothing. No one could get a rise out of me or make me nervous. I wasn't even nervous when I actually took the test. I was preternaturally calm. It even showed up on the video of the test—I looked half asleep! I guess cruising into the dojo with *September* and *Boogie Wonderland* in my head helped me keep my cool.

Then, in the summer of 2013, I prepared for my sandan test (third degree) and the band for that test was Apocalyptica, a band of cello players who started out doing Metallica covers. I didn't listen to the covers, but their original stuff, and particularly a song called *Broken Pieces*. Turns out *Broken Pieces* was a prescient choice. I went out three months before my test with an injury. I certainly felt like "broken pieces"! I didn't test that year.

"I'm broken pieces/pack up these pieces of me…"

Spring of 2014 and time to prepare for my sandan test again. I was not nervous, just...edgy. Not so edgy that I wanted to listen to anything very heavy, but I wasn't in the Earth, Wind and Fire mood either. I tried to relive the super relaxed feeling, but when I put on September, I ended up skipping it. I tried Depeche Mode again too, but that didn't work either. The band of choice instead was Lacuna Coil, a relatively heavy band with a male and a female singer.

A little heavy, a little edgy, but with positive lyrics. It felt like a good fit, but it wasn't perfect. I didn't need to listen to them like I had the other bands for the other two tests. My test didn't go as well as my previous two tests, at least in my mind. I wasn't as relaxed as I'd been with my nidan test, and I didn't feel it like I had with my shodan test. It wasn't that I hadn't prepared or wasn't ready. I had and I was. I wonder now if the edginess of my preparations and testing had something to do with the fact that I hadn't settled on a song or band. If I'd really found the magic band or song, would my test have gone smoother?

If I ever test again (which is so far away as to hardly worth mentioning), I'll know I absolutely have to find the right song for the test.

~2014

POSTURE IN AIKIDO

☯

In 2013 Mary Heiny Sensei visited our dojo for a weekend seminar. It was the first time I'd ever been to a seminar with her, and I really looked forward to it. I'd heard so much about her over the years, so before the seminar I took the time to watch a few videos of her doing aikido. What struck me then, and that I still admire and aspire to, is her incredible posture.

In three weeks, Mary Heiny Sensei, an amazing and highly respected sensei, will visit my dojo to give a seminar.

Heiny Sensei has been training for over 40 years. To me, that in itself is impressive enough—to be committed to a martial art is hard work. The training is physically, emotionally, and spiritually intense, so to do it for much of one's life is an extraordinary accomplishment. I wish I had something that I loved so much to devote my life to, like she and many other teachers have done.

What I like about Heiny Sensei, though, is her...stillness. When I watch her do aikido, I notice how still her body remains no matter what she does or who attacks her. She is in total control of herself and her partner. In the pictures and videos I've seen of O'Sensei, he looks exactly the same. He is the still point at the center in which his partners attack.

This stillness makes aikido efficient. The guys attacking

Heiny Sensei are quite a bit bigger than her, and yet she doesn't expend much energy dealing with them. She makes it look easy. Her body is relaxed and still; in fact it seems like she's barely engaged. The opposite must be happening, though. She has to be totally engaged, in the moment, and completely focused on what is happening in order for it to look so easy. If her focus was elsewhere, it wouldn't look so effortless.

I also like the way she initiates the movements. I've been working on that in my own practice lately, and it's difficult. How do I initiate the technique without being the aggressor? It's tricky. Heiny Sensei does it with ease. She makes small movements which draw her attacker out of his own space. Once he's out of his space and meeting her in that interstitial place where their two energies meet, she can do with him what she will. She's not rough because once he's in that space it is her responsibility to protect him. That's the aiki way.

The most important part of all of this is her posture. She's got incredible posture. No matter what she is doing, the integrity of her body stays intact. From the top of her head to her hips, her posture is impeccable. Heiny Sensei doesn't bend over or sway or get wobbly. She's always in complete control of her body. That is important in aikido.

If I'm in control of my own body, then I can be in control of my partner's body, and that is how we both stay safe. Unfortunately for me, the integrity of my posture breaks far too often. There are times when I feel myself losing control of my partner only to realize it is because I'm leaning to the side or bending over at the waist. This bending is because I'm leaning towards my partner, allowing myself to get sucked into his or her space. Once I do that, I am out of control, and I've given my partner my power.

What I learn from watching Heiny Sensei, and other teachers, including my own, is to keep my posture and my physical integrity.

~2013

UKEMI, POSTURE, AND LIFE

I wrote this a few months after that first Mary Heiny Sensei seminar still working on my issue with posture.

Posture...I've been thinking about it again.

This week during aikido class, I watched people do ukemi. Ukemi (oo-KEH-mee) is what we do when we fall or roll or get taken down into a pin. It is also the initial attack that precipitates the whole technique—someone has to attack in order to teach us how to handle that attack. It is so important in aikido it's called the "art of ukemi." We must practice the falling and rolling to keep ourselves safe. When I come charging in to attack my partner, I'd better be able to take a fall or roll, or I'm going to get hurt. So we practice ukemi. We roll and roll and take high falls.

As I watched people rolling, I paid attention to posture. I realized we have to maintain our perfect, controlled posture even in the midst of a roll or high fall. In fact, it seems even more important at that point, because in the midst of a pin or roll or high fall, we are vulnerable. Think about it. I'm flipping myself over in mid-air or I'm rolling on the ground. I am defenseless in that moment. The ONLY thing protecting me is my own presence of mind and body.

When I hit the ground again, or come up from the roll, I need to be in control of my body. It's crucial. Aikido is a martial art, and in order for it to remain martial, I need to be ready to get back up once I've hit the ground. That's how I protect myself, or how I come back to fight again.

One of the most important aspects of ukemi is that I have to be able to adjust...instantly. As an uke it is my job to attack my partner with energy and intention. It is my partner's job to blend with that and re-direct it. Once it's been re-directed, it is then my job to receive the change. This back and forth is what aikido is all about; it's the "joining together" represented by the "ai" in aikido. As uke, I have to be ready for anything. I may go in with a straight attack, but get spun completely around only to land on my back. To keep myself safe, I have to maintain control over myself, and I can do that through correct posture.

I can see all of this applying to my life outside of aikido. I need to be in control of myself because I certainly can't control what happens around me or what other people do. Things might change in an instant. I might go into a situation thinking it will turn out one way, only to be surprised and end up flat on my back (figuratively, of course!).

I have to maintain my emotional and energetic "posture." If I don't, then I end up floundering. I get blown around by life, rather than being in control of what I'm doing.

When a person has good physical posture, she preserves the integrity of her body. From her head down to her hips is one controlled line. It doesn't break or wobble. When people have good emotional and energetic "posture" the same thing happens—they keep their emotional integrity. They don't "break" that integrity, even when things get difficult or chaotic.

When we do aikido we practice under stress, because it strengthens us both physically and emotionally. Taking ukemi can be extremely stressful and scary. We attack our partners in order to help them with their aikido, but to do so we have to give our bodies to them. That can be scary, but it helps to learn how to do it correctly and with proper form so we keep ourselves safe.

Life can be stressful and chaotic and scary at times too. Keeping ourselves in alignment and maintaining our integrity might keep us safe. Practicing good "ukemi," learning how to fall and yet still come up fighting, may be the most important life lesson of all!

~2013

AIKIDO AND DANCE

I wrote this in 2011 when I prepared for my second degree (nidan) black belt test. A lot had happened since 2007 when I became a shodan.

> "Move like a beam of light;
> Fly like lightning,
> Strike like thunder,
> Whirl in circles around a stable center."
> ~O'Sensei

The above quote perfectly encapsulates how the past three years of dancing and practicing aikido have felt to me. I'd been a shodan for about two years when I decided I needed a break from aikido. My practice felt a little stagnant, and I felt a little lost. I couldn't put it into words, so I didn't really discuss it with anyone in the dojo. I didn't feel physically or mentally prepared to keep moving forward in my aikido practice. If aikido is a "do" or a "way" then I'd lost sight of my way.

At this time a friend of mine was involved with a local Afro-Brazilian dance and drum group. She'd talked to me about the dance class that was open to the community—raved about it is more exact. She tried to talk me into joining the class. I did not feel comfortable dancing in an unfamiliar dance style...in public. But the day came when it was her birthday and she asked me to come to class again, and I couldn't refuse because, well, it was her birthday.

I knew I'd found a place where I could be comfortable

because I saw the lead drummer and the group's director bow before he entered the room. Truth is, I too, quietly and unobtrusively bowed before I stepped on to the raised dance floor. I couldn't explain why other than habit. However, when I asked the director later (on another night) about why he bowed before entering the room, he explained that he thought of the dance and drum space as sacred.

Clearly, I'd come to the right place.

I discovered I loved this style of dance, loved the rhythms of the drums, and loved the way I felt after class. I started going to dance class every week. There came a point where I realized that my focus was this dance and drum group, not aikido. I thought long and hard about what to do because I couldn't do them both, and decided that since I was feeling lost in aikido anyway, I'd take a break and dance instead. I knew the break was temporary. I knew in my heart I'd return to aikido.

I was gone for 1 1/2 years.

The funny thing is, aikido kept popping up in my dance. I never thought a martial art and the art of dance would have anything in common. I couldn't have been more wrong. Dancing and aikido "blend" well. The first time this came to light was when I did a workshop with a guest teacher. I was new to this style of dance but was convinced to go (much like we tell new aikido students to attend seminars with visiting teachers no matter their rank). The dance she taught was an Orixa (Oreesha) dance, which was based on the gods brought to Brazil from Africa. This particular dance was a representation of the god Ogum who is a god of war, iron, and blacksmiths. He is portrayed carrying a machete. The first move she taught was Ogum cutting with a machete. It was remarkably similar to the yokomen uchi strike! We were also supposed to "channel" the energy of this war god into our dancing, meaning an intensity and preciseness in our movements. We were supposed to be warriors. I could handle that. My friend told me I picked up the moves quickly. I told her they were like aikido.

After that experience, I noticed aikido in much of my dancing. I learned to samba and found that the steps in samba kept my feet in hanmi. I learned a basic salsa step and laughed because it was a similar movement to the hasso—hips up and then hips back with a nice little swing. Whenever we danced any of the warrior or hunter Orixa's I fell immediately into an aikido mindset. When I'd dance I'd find my hands in front of my center and when a move was difficult or fast or both I'd drop my weight and focus on my center.

I also found a type of ukemi in my dance classes. In this style of dance, the dancers move in lines of three or four people across the floor up to the drummers. We engage in a conversation with the drummers. The dancers communicate with the drummers and the drummers communicate with the dancers. I've had the privilege to be on both sides of that conversation and it's a beautiful experience. There is a point when I am moving across the floor towards a drummer and I make contact with him/her. It doesn't necessarily mean eye contact, but a connection with a particular rhythm a particular drum is playing. My body connects to that rhythm and moves to it. Sometimes the drummer picks up on the connection and we move and play in harmony.

That is a true aiki moment, a coming together of our two energies. It feels to me like I feel when I take ukemi and there is a real connection between nage and uke. It's a beautiful feeling.

There is also a connection between all the dancers in my line. We are supposed to dance together. We move up towards the drummers together, we try not to break our line with someone lagging behind or surging ahead, and we try to do the choreography in perfect sync. I can feel it when it works. There have been moments when we all dance in harmony. There are times when we would connect as dancer to dancer and dancer to drummer, and I would think later about the meaning of the word "ai" from aikido. We often call it harmony but I like the definition of "joining together" better. It better fits the action of two people—nage and uke, dancer and dancer, dancer and drummer, drummer and drummer—joining together to meet in one unified sphere, even if it's only for a moment.

I danced two or three times a week for that 1 1/2 years. But there came a point when it was time to return to aikido. I found myself talking about and relating everything in dance to aikido. I couldn't focus; did I want to dance or drum? If I drum, which drum? I was all over the place. My friend who got me into the group said she recognized my restlessness as a need to get back to aikido. I did too. So back to aikido I went!

My aikido was not the same when I came back, not at all. There were classes when I did tai no henko and wondered whose body I was in. It didn't feel the same. I didn't feel the same as when I left. It was to be expected, of course. In many ways, I liked the way I changed. My body felt more relaxed and I felt a greater connection to the ground. My hips were definitely more relaxed because they got worked a lot in dance classes. I'd go to a dance class and samba one night and then go to aikido the next night. My hips were definitely loose. The change was internal too. I didn't feel as wound up inside when I'd do a technique but instead felt a sense of having unraveled a little bit. It was nice.

There were a couple of areas in aikido in which I struggled. My aiki weapons were not very good when I came back. Where my open hand techniques seemed to be able to handle the time away, my weapons did not. My sword strikes were sloppy. When I worked with the jo, my hands were constantly out of place and falling off. It was disconcerting to me because I love aiki weapons. The only thing to do, of course, was to practice. I'd practice sword strikes before class to re-familiarize myself with the weapon. Same with the jo. It eventually started to fall into place. Honestly, it is still a work in progress.

The other area in which I struggled was that my hips and lower back were too loose! I'd come to class and Robinson Sensei would notice that my lower back was too arched, and as soon as she told me, I'd feel how the arching was making me weak. I couldn't handle a strong attack by uke with my back arched—I was easy to push over. I worked hard to be aware of and to correct this arch in my lower back. I could feel my strength when I'd make the correction. I'd also work hard to make sure my upper body was straight and aligned with the earth. Then I'd go to a dance class and be told to stick out my butt and move my upper body like a snake! It's been a challenge, to say the least, to balance the two energies and styles.

One of the ways in which it all comes together for me is with energy. Of course, ki is a major part of aikido, so much that it is a part of the name. Ki is usually defined as "life energy." The dance group to which I belonged was called Batucaxe (bah-too-kah-shay). Batucaxe, like Aikido, is a word made from different words. In this instance, "batuca" which means the beat and "axe" (ah-shay) which means...life energy or life force. Some of the dance moves are designed to generate "axe" in much the same way as our aikido moves generate ki. When we dance we lift our arms to the sky and then drop down in a low crouch to connect with the earth. We reach up to the sky to grab lightning and then strike it down on the ground, and when I do this I can't help but think of the energy of ken suburi three—reaching up with the bokken to take in the sky energy and then striking it down.

Aikido and dance. Ki and axe. It's all about energy and movement. It's all about connecting with the world around us and with the people around us. There is a Batucaxe song called *Let it Out* done to one of my favorite rhythms, and when I hear these lyrics I think of aikido:

"Let it out, let it out, let it in/Just surrender or you're never gonna win/You've got to take a chance, move your body and dance, Everybody feel good together."

And as O'Sensei said in *The Art of Peace*:

"Your mind should be in harmony with the functioning of the universe; your body should be in tune with the movement of the universe; body and mind should be bound as one, unified with the activity of the universe."

Ultimately everyone is in harmony with the universe, and everyone is feeling good together.

~2011

THIS IS WHERE YOU LIVE

**I had been working with a beginner who seemed
impatient at not being able to do what I or the other
black belts could do. She kept jumping in over her
head. I recognized the impatience, because I have
seen it before, and I even felt it. Not long after that, I
watched the movie Hitch and one of my favorite
movie scenes made me think of aikido and beginners.**

In the movie *Hitch* with Will Smith and Kevin James,
Hitch, played by Will Smith, is the "Date Doctor," a
man who hires himself out to help other men get dates
with women, often unattainable women. Albert, played by
Kevin James, is such a man, shy, clumsy, and awkward. He
wants the beautiful, rich, and famous Allegra. In one scene
Albert tells Hitch that dancing is one area he does not worry
about when it comes to women. He thinks he has moves.
With a questioning look, Hitch asks Albert to show him
what he means. Hitch puts on music and what follows is
one of the funniest scenes in film.

Hitch's advice to Albert made me think of helping
beginners in aikido. Albert did not need any wild moves to
dance, and aikido beginners do not need fancy moves to
progress. When we start in aikido, everything is so awkward
and strange, we don't know which foot goes where or what
to do with our hands. We are timid and try to make as few
mistakes as possible. On the other hand, we also watch the
advanced students, the black belts, and we see how they fly

around the dojo, we observe their confidence and their ability to know where to step and what their hands are supposed to do. To a beginner, the advanced students look like Will Smith dancing.

So...as beginners, we want to emulate the advanced students and try things beyond our abilities. We want to fly so we attempt to breakfall when we're not ready. We want to show that we have confidence so we go charging in to attack one of the advanced students and find ourselves crashing to the mat.

My advice to beginners. Take it slow. Yes, watch the advanced students. Observe what they do and how they do it. Take the steps and train so you can do what they do...one day. But don't try to do it all at once or before your body is trained in the correct form. Don't try to prove you can handle it or that you are strong enough to take it.

As Hitch said, "you is a fluid concept right now." As beginners, we are learning, changing, and growing. Fluid.

Stick with the basics. "This is where you live."

~2015

TRUE EMPTINESS

In our AikidoKids! classes, one of the perks of good behavior on the mat is to pick a quote from The Art of Peace to put on the whiteboard that hangs on the wall. We then read the quote and discuss it in our circle time after class. The teachers ask the kids what they think a certain quote or phrase or word means. The quotes also make me think! This essay came after one of the kids posted the following quote.

> "If you have not
> Linked yourself
> To true emptiness,
> You will never understand
> The Art of Peace."
> ~O'Sensei, The Art of Peace

I've been contemplating what the phrase "linked yourself to true emptiness" means in this poem, at least in an aikido context, for over a week.

What is "true emptiness"? Is it a feeling? A moment? And how does it relate to the Art of Peace that O'Sensei practiced and handed down to aikido practitioners?

For me, true emptiness, as he writes of it here, is a moment in time and space. It is the transition time, the point at which one person either takes the balance of another or one person loses her balance. When I am taking ukemi, when I am the person attacking and being thrown, there is a moment, usually brief, when I've begun to lose my balance, and I can feel myself falling. If I give myself to that moment, that space of falling, then my mind becomes blank and all I experience is that space in which I am no longer in control of my body, but I am at the mercy of gravity. The trick is to give myself to that moment fully, to experience it, and to not fight it.

It is a third space, neither standing nor falling, neither balanced nor completely unbalanced; it is the time and space in between. It is also a space where there is no thought, hence the "emptiness."

It reminds me of the feeling I got swinging as a child. I'd go so high the chain would become slack, and there was the moment when the swing and I would hang for a brief fraction of time before we swung back towards the ground. I loved that feeling. Still do.

So, maybe that is the true emptiness. It is the interstitial space when I am giving myself over to my body to transition from one space to another, from one moment to another, from one type of consciousness to another. When I give myself to that space, I lose my conscious thought and simply become my body, only feeling the movement, not thinking of it. Whether I'm the person doing the throw or the person being thrown, I can still give myself to that space. If I am throwing, I can step back from conscious thought and blend with my partner's energy and allow that energy to be transformed into something new.

I do not know if this is what O'Sensei meant when he said to understand the Art of Peace, I have to understand "true emptiness," but perhaps the meaning of true emptiness and how we link that to the Art of Peace is up to all of us to find for ourselves. For me, it is the empty in-between space.

~2015

THE LANGUAGE WE USE

A ikido, of course, is a martial art. But it is also the martial art that concerns itself with harmony and peace. That's why I believe we need to be mindful of the language we use when training and teaching.

Words have power.

I noticed one day while teaching that I told my uke to grab me "harder." As soon as I said it, I realized that "hard" was not what I meant. Grabbing hard could mean squeezing without any kind of engagement. Uke's grab my wrist "hard" all the time! What I really wanted my partner to do was to grab my wrist firmly so that he made a connection to me.

It got me thinking about what other words or phrases people tend to use in aikido that could be changed to open up more peaceful possibilities.

Several of the high ranked sensei's to whose seminars I've attended rarely use the word "attacker" when talking about the uke. They use the word "partner." It makes a difference! My mindset as nage is much different if I think of the person coming in with a strike or punch or grab as my partner and not my attacker. If he is my partner, that means we are working together and not in opposition. He is giving me the strike or grab or punch to aid me with my aikido. He's not there to lock me down and give me a hard time. He's my partner, not my enemy.

Aikido people can also get hung up on the idea that they will throw their partner. To throw my partner implies that I am striving to do something to him, to make him move and fall. It's aggressive and oppositional. It's like telling my partner, "I will make you do this." Not many of us enjoy being told what to do and being forced into a throw or fall is the physical equivalent of that. Focusing on the throw is also focusing on the end result and not the process. If I focus on the throw and that I will "throw you," then I've skipped ahead to the end, and I have not paid attention to my partner in the beginning or the middle. Often when I do that, the blend is weak, and I resort to trying to force my partner into the technique. When I focus on throwing my partner, I am doing aikido to him, not with him.

Then there is the language about "grabbing" or "capturing" or "taking" our uke's center and balance. Those words by themselves are combative and confrontational. When I hear that on the mat, I automatically put up invisible barriers around my center, and if I do that, then how can I do aikido with my partner? If I'm protecting my center against my partner's attempt to "take" it, then we can't do aikido fully. I'm not really present in the interaction if a big part of me has been locked down and hidden away.

Instead, I like to think of it as engaging with my partner's center and disrupting his balance. I'm not taking something from my partner, I'm simply disrupting it, like ripples on the surface of water when a stone drops in. It's like when we do an atemi to unbalance our partner without actually making contact. It makes uke lighter and easier to move without injury.

I like it when my partner wants to engage with me. I don't mind when my partner tries to disrupt my balance. That's fine. That's fun!

In my practice and in my teaching, I'm being mindful of the language I use to describe aikido and what we are trying to accomplish on and off the mat. Just like with the physical practice of aikido, the words I use need to convey the peaceful intent of aikido.

~2017

ANTICIPATION ON AND OFF THE MAT

A nticipation. We often think of it positively, like a child getting excited about a birthday or holiday, or an adult looking forward to a big event. But there is a downside to anticipation—prediction. To anticipate something is also to predict what is going to happen, and that can be unhealthy and even dangerous.

My aikido dojo is hosting a visiting teacher this weekend, and I've been anticipating this seminar for a long time. I'm looking forward to it! But, as the person in charge of organization and marketing, I find myself anticipating in another way...predicting. Every so often I sit at my desk and make tick marks of how many people I expect to come to the seminar. The success of this seminar has been on my mind constantly for the past few days.

I finally told myself I'd do no more anticipating. Whatever happens this weekend, happens. There is nothing more I can do.

The worst thing about this kind of anticipation (well, any anticipation) is it takes me out of the moment. I can't enjoy the present moment when I am either looking forward to something that will happen in the future or trying to predict what will happen in the future. It's all focused on the future.

I began to relate this aspect of anticipation to my aikido practice. In short, I should NEVER anticipate in aikido, either as the attacker or as the person being attacked. It happens all the time, though. It is understandable since an aikido class or seminar is arranged around the teacher demonstrating a technique and then the students performing that specific technique. How can I not anticipate what is coming when the teacher has just said the name of the technique and the attack?

However, I think there is a difference between knowing what attack will come and anticipating how it will come. Every single moment in aikido (as in life) is different from the moment before or after. I may have done a particular technique a thousand times, and I may have worked with my partner hundreds of times, but it is still different in that moment. My partner will be different in that moment. His attack will be different. It may be harder or softer or off center a little or any millions of variations. I will be a different person in that moment than I was the last time we did this technique together. The variables within the dojo will be different.

Because of this, it is important for me not to anticipate. I need to be in that moment if I want to do things correctly, and, more importantly, if I want to stay safe and keep my partner safe. If I'm anticipating that he will strike at me hard, and I react accordingly, but what he really does is give me an attack much softer than normal, my reaction is out of balance. If I anticipate his soft attack as something hard, then I could act more aggressively than is necessary and hurt him.

If I'm not in the present moment, I can't feel my partner's energy, so we lose our connection. The connection is what aikido is all about. After all, the incoming energy is why we always work with partners. Aikido doesn't work without connection. My connection is faulty if I'm anticipating and predicting what my partner will do.

If I'm the person doing the attacking, then I have to work to keep from anticipating and predicting as well. How can I give an honest and meaningful attack if I'm thinking I know exactly what my partner will do next? If I know what he will do, I might as well not keep training. It becomes a dance with choreographed steps. The beauty of taking ukemi is that you are constantly engaged on a moment-by-moment basis with your partner. You go in hard with a punch or strike, but then you have to meld softly with whatever happens to your body as your partner takes control of the situation.

I remember vividly a time when I attacked one of my teachers and predicted what he was going to do. He was teaching a technique and held out his hand in a way I'd seen many times before. I smiled thinking I knew exactly how he was going to throw me. Luckily for me, his technique was so good, so fast, and so hard, I didn't have time to realize he wasn't doing what I expected, until I was on my back on the floor! If he hadn't been so controlled, I might have been injured...and it would have been all my fault. If I'd had time to think, "Hey, this isn't what he's supposed to be doing!" I likely would have seized up, tensed up, and hurt myself.

That was a good lesson for on the mat and off. Anticipation and predicting will take me out of the moment, and that is not where I need to be. I need to be right here, right now, paying attention to what I'm doing and to what others are doing around me. That is how I keep myself safe and sane!

~2011

AIKIDO AND A GARDEN HOSE

☯

"Spiritual power. Not muscle power" ~*Saotome Shihan*

Aikido is not about physical power. At least, it is not supposed to be. When you watch a high-level teacher practicing aikido, it often looks fake. The reason it looks fake is that he is not using physical power. He doesn't block or parry or meet force with force. He is being gentle.

It sounds strange to talk about being gentle in a martial art. To me, though, it makes perfect sense. When I am gentle, I can make a real connection with my partner. I can't do that if I am tense or aggressive, because then I am only focused on myself and not my partner. I can only feel my own tension, and I can only think about my own aggression. This all gets in the way of my connection—it's interference.

Imagine an ordinary garden hose. Now imagine it cold, constricted, and crimped—tense. How does the water flow out of it? It's restricted, slow; it comes out in spurts, and when you see the water spurting out at the nozzle, it is jagged and uneven. Now imagine that same water hose warmed by the sun, completely stretched out, and full of water. How does the water flow out now? Even, smooth, and full of energy.

I imagine my own aikido power in terms of that hose. I don't want my energy crimped and restricted. I want it full and flowing. I can do this by keeping myself energized with "spiritual power," by releasing tension and aggression from my body and my mind.

When I train without tension I can make a genuine connection with my partner. When my partner grabs me or strikes at me, I can sincerely connect with her. My energy is flowing outward, like a hose, trying to make a connection and understand what is happening with her. Only then can I do something, and even then I'm not making something happen—I'm allowing something to happen.

Making aikido happen is "muscle power," the cold, crimped up hose. Allowing aikido to happen in the moment, when I am relaxed and free from aggression is "spiritual power."

~2011

ENERGETIC BATTERIES

☯

Aikido is energy training. The name itself speaks of this energy; the "ki" in aiKIdo means energy or life force. Put together, the word ai-ki-do means "the way of joining energy" or "the way of harmony." I recently spent a weekend at a seminar with Hiroshi Ikeda Shihan, a 7th-degree black belt, who teaches "internal power" movements. Ikeda Shihan can do all of the physical aikido techniques, throws, and joint locks that we all see in demonstrations, but he also teaches internal power, the stuff you don't see. We spent the entire weekend working with this internal energy, practicing moving our partners using only small shifts in our bodies and the intention of our minds.

After eight hours of intense internal energy aikido practice over the weekend, I thought I'd be exhausted on Monday. The opposite happened. I felt great. I went about my regular daily schedule with vigor. That evening I taught the kids aikido class and had infinite amounts of patience! I attended my regular adult aikido class and felt more grounded and centered than I have felt in a long, long time.

If that wasn't enough, I went to a dance class with West African drummers. During the high energy class, I couldn't stop moving. I danced the choreography, and even when it wasn't my turn, I danced off to the side and in the back. I had so much energy; it felt like it was exploding out of me. I could have danced all night.

That got me thinking...did I accumulate energy over the

weekend during my aikido training? Was I then using that energy to fuel myself during dance class?

Am I a battery?

If so, did I tap into some external energy, like The Force?

It felt to me as if I'd been plugged in, charged up, and then I'd used that harnessed energy the next day. Unfortunately, like a battery, I ran out of juice. The next time I went to an aikido class and we played around with the "internal energy" we'd learned over the weekend, I had nothing left. I was empty, running only on fumes. My battery had been depleted and I needed to recharge.

I think about all of the energy out in the world, in the universe. Infinite amounts of energy. I'd like to plug my battery into that energy and charge up!

~2016

INTENSIVE TRAINING

M y aikido dojo is holding an intensive training seminar called a gasshuku. Intensive means all day and without much time for breaks. 7 am to 5 pm- -1/2 hour for breakfast and 1/2 hour for lunch. Small little breaks in between each hour, but only to get a drink of water and a bit of fruit or something. Honestly, there is barely enough time to use the bathroom!

This all-day intensive training is completely exhausting.

Exhaustion is one purpose of this intensive training. The theory: you get so physically and mentally drained that the techniques sink in. You get beyond the point of trying to do anything so it all just...happens. Allowing things to happen is the best way to learn. When doing aikido or any physical activity, you should not be thinking but doing and allowing the activity to happen.

What makes the gasshuku so much fun is that we have a different teacher each hour. All of the black belts teach for an hour. It's wonderful to see and hear what they each have to offer. This change of teachers is one of the reasons the gasshuku is so tiring. We all train with one teacher and get used to that teacher and her way of teaching. So, to have someone else teach in a different way and with their own twist on the techniques makes it difficult. Rewarding, but difficult.

This year we are particularly lucky because we have two visiting teachers from another style of aikido. Not only do we get a different teacher, but the way they do aikido will be a little different from the way we do it at our dojo. And, it's always fun to learn something new.

I love this day of training. I love doing aikido until I feel like collapsing on the mat (and believe me, we all collapse on the mat at the end of the day). The intensive training can take me to another level of aikido; I might physically learn a new technique, or I might emotionally grasp an aspect of aikido that has eluded me.

One year we spent one full hour practicing high-falls. Different ways of practicing high falls, different ways of doing high-falls, and then fall after fall after fall. The next day I woke up feeling like I'd been hit by a truck. But, it was a huge help and I felt much better about my ability to take those falls.

Regardless of whether I learn something new or not, I've spent the day doing aikido which is what I love to do. I get to spend the day with my fellow aikido mates. To me, that's a day well spent!

~2010

THE MURK

Is it necessary to have clarity in my aikido practice? It feels like I should. If feels like I should have something to work and focus on every time I step onto the mat. I don't. For two months I was sick and didn't practice, and perhaps that long break has knocked me off my game. Not only am I not experiencing clarity, but I also don't feel confident about my practice, like I don't know what I'm doing. I know my aikido practice goes in fits and spurts, has peaks and valleys, and that—even after all these years—I struggle with some of the techniques. I know that on some days a technique like shiho nage will come easily, and on other days it will be the hardest technique I've ever done.

Now everything feels murky and clouded. Part of me wants to fight my way out of it, but another part wants to let the murk clear on its own. I heard that if you find yourself stuck in quicksand you should not fight, but relax, and the relaxation will buoy your body up to the surface. If you fight, of course, you'll get sucked under. The relaxation and letting go of the need to control what is happening is what allows you to float to the top and to safety.

So that's what I will do. I will let go and relax and allow the cloudiness to disperse on its own. I won't force it. Who knows? Maybe what crystallizes will be something amazing.

~2015

INTELLECTUALIZING ON THE MAT

☯

Another early essay

"As soon as you see something, you already start to intellectualize it. As soon as you intellectualize something, it is no longer what you saw." ~ Shunryu Suzuki-roshi (1905-1971).

In my aikido practice, I experience this regularly both in my own training and when I listen to and work with others. However, it is not something we "see" and then intellectualize so much as something we experience and then intellectualize. Aikido is a difficult martial art (as I suppose they all are), and we learn dozens of techniques from lots of different attacks and with different ways of moving. Of course, we see the techniques as they are demonstrated by our teacher, but we then have to feel them and learn them in contact with another person, our partners in practice.

What I experience and hear in the dojo is the moment when one of us "sees" the technique and lets out a "Yes!" or "I got it" or "That's it!" To me, that is the moment when we start to intellectualize whatever it is we've learned. Once we intellectualize what we've learned or "got," then we take ourselves out of the present moment of awareness.

As Suzuki said, as soon as we intellectualize what we've gotten, understood or seen, "it is no longer what you saw." If I'm practicing an aikido technique, and at the precise moment I understand it at some level, I verbalize I've gotten it, then whatever it is I've gotten changes. It jumps from my body's feeling that I've done something right to an intellectual analysis and understanding. I've jumped from a body awareness to being in my head. I have to be in my head to yell out "That's it!" Aikido is a physical practice and all physical endeavors are best left to the body. There is a time and place to intellectualize your practice, but the time is not when you are actually doing it. The time to think about aikido or talk about aikido is off the mat, not on it.

It is important to be fully present and aware at every moment in any physical activity, but particularly in a dangerous martial art that has the ability to inflict pain and damage. When I do certain techniques, I am in the position to break an arm, so if I think about whether I've "gotten" it, I'm not thinking about my partner. My partner, and my connection to my partner, should be the focus of my attention, not whether I got the technique.

There is also the problem of intellectualizing too early in the process. It's like editing in writing. If I edit what I'm writing while I'm in the midst of a thought, then I can ruin the thought or idea. I need to wait until I'm done and then do the editing...the intellectualizing. If I'm doing an aikido technique and all of sudden I've got it and say something, then I've hijacked the entire process. If I stop and dwell on the "eureka" moment, then I stop the forward momentum. What if I was going to keep learning and understanding at a deep level an aspect of that technique? By stopping in mid-stream and giving attention to the understanding, I've stopped any further understanding that may have happened further along.

I've experienced moments in aikido, beautiful moments, where I've come to some understanding of a technique or application and fully experienced it in the moment. I didn't think about it or remark on it. I felt it. I felt it all the way from that moment to the end. It is only in those moments that I've learned something. I didn't intellectualize it so it didn't change.

That moment of awareness in my body stayed in my body, and so I was able to hold onto it forever.

~2010

ENGAGED RATHER THAN
ATTACHED

☯

**Hans Goto Shihan, 7th dan, is my teacher's teacher.
Every year he comes to Tucson to teach a weekend-
long seminar.**

At one of his seminars, Goto Sensei said there is a difference between being engaged and being attached. When he said this, it was one of those "a-ha" moments I get regularly in aikido. It is a great distinction.

Engagement vs. Attachment. Once again I found a life lesson on the aikido mat.

So, what is the difference? My thoughts are that in aikido, we have all experienced the uke who grabs so hard it feels like all your circulation will be cut off. He latches on and squeezes, but doesn't actually do anything other than hold on tight. There is no connection with you as a partner. That is attachment. His hand is attached to your wrist, but he is not engaged in the attack or with you. That requires more than simply latching on. When uke simply attaches, then nage doesn't really need to even do aikido. There is no energy coming towards you, and there is no attempt to disrupt your center.

There have been many times when I've been on the mat, frustrated because my partner grabs onto me and then plants his feet like a toddler who doesn't want to leave the park. That's not engagement. That's not honestly giving me an attack. It's an attempt to say, "Ha-ha, I can lock you down and you can't move me."

Engagement as an uke is what I think teachers mean when they say to "give an honest attack." Uke is actively engaged with nage. Uke gives himself to nage, his body, and his spirit. That's where the "ai" in aikido shows up—joining together. When uke is engaged, the attack moves and changes. He keeps the attack coming and keeps in constant contact with nage, not only to be aware of openings he can exploit, but to keep himself safe.

I must do the same thing as nage. If I get tense and grab my partner and my focus is on throwing him or moving him, then I'm not really engaged. I'm attached. It's not just my physical body that's attached, but my spirit. When I've attached myself to my partner, I've given him my power.

If I'm engaged, I have a nice, firm grasp on my partner, but I'm not latched on and my focus is soft. When I'm engaged, I am relaxed, so my initial blend is much smoother and more effective. The relaxed engagement allows me to move quickly and decisively to get into a safe position. Engagement—being relaxed and feeling what my partner is doing, rather than forcing my partner to do something.

We hear in aikido that we do aikido with our partner, not to our partner. To me, this is the essence of the attachment vs. engagement. Attachment is doing aikido to your partner. It is concern only for a result. Engagement is doing aikido with your partner. It is concerned with listening to your partner, and the result will occur naturally.

This all applies to my daily life too. It is easy to get caught up in how good I am at something and the result I want. I get attached. I get attached to how I think I should be, or how I'd like my partner to be, or how I'd like a technique to turn out. That doesn't help me. It's unhealthy. It's harder to be engaged, but much more fulfilling—to be engaged and enjoy the process—to listen to everyone, to blend and be in the right place so projects fall into place.

When I'm engaged in life rather than attached to what

happens in my life, I can more easily give up things, projects, and people who are not helping or being supportive. But, it's a process.

Attachment or engagement. I choose to be engaged.

~2017

JOY IN TRAINING

"Always practice the Art of Peace in a vibrant and joyful manner."
~Morihei Ueshiba.

One of the aspects of aikido I love is the joy expressed in our training. The first time I ever stepped foot in my dojo, I was terrified. That terror was quickly dispelled when I saw the smiling faces of almost everyone in the dojo, even during training—especially during training. I thought it was odd. Smiles in a martial arts dojo? Shouldn't they all be serious? After all, in the dojo, you learn how to fight and do potential damage to another person. They shouldn't be smiling!

However, as I trained and studied aikido, I began to understand the smiles. It's not out of a lack of seriousness (well, sometimes it can be a lack of seriousness), but an expression of all O'Sensei taught. He believed that love was the ultimate expression of a warrior and aikido...not killing someone or doing damage to this person. Love. When we smile in the dojo during practice, it is because we've discovered something in our practice or in ourselves that makes us smile.

I've experienced many moments of joy on the mat. When I take ukemi, I like to savor the moment right after my partner breaks my balance and before I fall. I'm hanging on to a brief moment in time, like falling in slow motion. I can feel the exact moment when I lose my balance, and then I can feel the exact moment when I start to fall.

I love that moment. It makes me smile. I'm serious when I'm attacking my partner, because I know I'll likely get thrown into a roll or high-fall or pinned to the ground. When I get up from the mat, though, I smile. Sometimes I laugh. It's exhilarating.

I feel like I'm experiencing, in my own small way, training in a joyful manner.

~2013

TRANSITIONS

ow do you handle transitions? Are they easy for you? Do you move from one job or activity or phase of life with grace, or are you like me and get pulled so hard in two directions, clinging to the past and desiring the future, that you feel you might break?

When my son was little, I read parenting books that told me to ease into transitions to make life easier for both child and parent. When it was time to leave the park, give the child plenty of warning, start packing up slowly, say goodbye to everyone, so the pang of leaving would be minimized. Sometimes it worked. Sometimes it didn't. Some days it was better to pull up stakes and leave right away, like ripping the bandage off quickly. Over, done, move on.

When I dance or do aikido, I love those transitional moments. I look forward to them, and I allow myself to savor that moment of falling when I take ukemi, or when I break my partner's balance, or the moment in the choreography when one dance move follows another. Transitions in dance can be so, so sweet, like biting into a ripe juicy peach. One move falls seamlessly into the next, like slipping into a pool of water. It's a supremely joyful moment.

In aikido, when I let go and allow myself to feel the

transition, the moment my partner takes my balance and I can no longer hang on to it, it feels like touching a piece of the infinite. To let go and feel that space, where you are neither hanging on nor crashing to the ground, is incredibly liberating, freeing, and life-affirming.

I wish I could do that in my mundane life. In life, transitions are painful wracking contractions. It is unfortunate, too, because that's what life is! Life is a constant series of transitions. Most are small and relatively easy to maneuver, but the others, the big ones, those are not so easy. At least, not for me. I wish I could allow them to happen, to feel when it's time to let go of one part of my life, to experience it until it's done, and then drop into the next part without hesitation and struggle.

In aikido, I've learned when it's time to take the fall, that in order to protect myself, I have to hit the mat. Sometimes my partner is rough and I have to bail out early; sometimes my partner is strong but firm, and I can relax into the technique, waiting until the last moment to fall because I feel protected.

If only I could see life in such straightforward terms. If it is rough and hurting me, leave. Protect myself. Take the fall. Roll away. If it is going well, follow the path for as long as it takes me where I want to go. Then leave. The difference is that in daily life, I come up frustrated and in aikido I come up smiling, ready to try again.

In dance, I've learned to absorb the rhythms of the drums to hear when it's time to transition from one move to another. Transitions in dance have taught me to not stop my momentum in preparation to change but to continue on with the flow of the movement. That is until it is time to stop. Then I stop, full out. Perhaps I need to discover a universal rhythm, something I can tap into, so I know when it is time to change to the next experience. If I do, then perhaps I can also learn how to handle life's transitions with more ease and grace.

~2016

THE MAN OR WOMAN IN THE ARENA

☯

I've been contemplating this quote by Theodore Roosevelt for the past couple of days:

"It is not the critic who counts; not the man who points out how the strong man stumbles, or where the doer of deeds could have done them better. The credit belongs to the man who is actually in the arena, whose face is marred by dust and sweat and blood; who strives valiantly; who errs, who comes short again and again, because there is no effort without error and shortcoming; but who does actually strive to do the deeds; who knows great enthusiasms, the great devotions; who spends himself in a worthy cause; who at the best knows in the end the triumph of high achievement, and who at the worst, if he fails, at least fails while daring greatly, so that his place shall never be with those cold and timid souls who neither know victory nor defeat."

I've been lucky in that I have a lot of supportive people in my life as I "strive to do the deeds." My friends and family have been there for me as I've progressed in aikido, performed as a dancer, and began the long journey of writing a novel. I hope I've been supportive and not a critic for my friends who have gone back to school, started their own businesses, written novels, and began new ventures. All around me I see people being supportive of each other.

There is another part of the quote that speaks to me, that in the end, it's better to have dared greatly and failed than to never have tried in the first place. There have been times during my aikido career when I felt like quitting (of course, there was the period when I did quit, but I came back), or have been too tired or busy to go to class, or when I've been injured and could not train. The injuries were the worst, especially when they've been bad enough to keep me out for several weeks, or in one case, several months. It is those times when I wonder if it is worth it, the effort, the frustration, the pain. On days when my old injuries bother me, when my joints ache, or when my neck is stiff, I think, no. I can't keep doing this forever. On other days, when aikido feels like magic, when I feel like I've touched a fundamental aspect of human nature, or when I feel at peace on the mat, then I think, yes, of course, it is worth it.

Whether I keep on going or not, I at least got into the arena and dared. That is something I will never regret.

~2014

THE AIKIDO HERO'S JOURNEY

"Every hero must have the courage to be alone, to take the journey for himself." Joseph Campbell

Over the years I have studied Joseph Campbell's work concerning the hero's journey. It's incredible stuff! He discovered that the story of the hero is similar across many cultures and over thousands of years. Because of this similarity, the hero's journey is universal. One aspect of the hero's journey is it need not be an actual hero like we see in the ancient stories or even in some of our modern stories, like *Star Wars* or *Harry Potter*, although we enjoy these bigger-than-life stories.

The hero can be anyone and everyone. The hero's journey is our human journey as well. The "hero" is us.

One night our dojo had brown belt testing, and I watched as the woman testing sat on the bench in the back of the dojo and studied her notebook. She was likely looking over what techniques she had to do that night to make sure she had them clear in her mind. It was a poignant moment. Even though there were plenty of people on the mat, she was alone.

I then realized that we all go through our own hero's journey when we practice aikido. What struck me has to do with Campbell's quote above, that the hero must take the journey alone. We can have teachers and mentors and friends along the way, but in the end, when it comes down to performing, we have to do it alone. We have to stand in the middle of the mat, before our teacher and sometimes an entire board of teachers, and we have to show we know our aikido.

This is especially true with dan testing. As my teacher says, "it takes a dojo" to get a dan candidate prepared for a test, but for the actual test you are out there alone except for your uke. You have to prove yourself. You have to attain the rank on your own merits.

There are several steps to the hero's journey.

1. Call to Adventure
2. Refusal of the Call
3. Supernatural Aid (meeting a mentor)
4. Crossing the Threshold
5. Belly of the Whale
6. Road of Trials
7. Meeting with the Goddess
8. Temptation
9. Atonement with the Father
10. Apotheosis
11. The Ultimate Boon
12. Refusal of the Return
13. Magic Flight
14. Rescue from Without
15. Return
16. Master of Two Worlds
17. Freedom to Live

The steps the hero must take are ones we take in our everyday lives, although we rarely think of them in terms of us being "heroes." It is simply life. At some point in our lives, around the teenage years (why do you think so many of the mythic heroes are teenagers when they are "called"?), we get a call to leave our homes and families and go off into the world. We might meet a mentor or teacher or an older friend who helps us along the way.

This all happens in aikido, only in a more condensed way. We get our Call to Adventure when we decide to join a dojo. We meet a mentor in our teacher and also in our sempai. We cross a threshold to begin the training.

In the movies, this step, Crossing the Threshold, is usually very dramatic. Think of Dorothy in the *Wizard of Oz* when she opens the door of her house into the Land of Oz. The world she leaves behind is black and white and the world she enters is color. It's a magical moment and clearly shows how the heroine is moving from an ordinary world into a new, unknown world.

In aikido, we treat thresholds with great respect. We bow when entering the dojo and when crossing over onto the training mat. We recognize that we are leaving behind our mundane world and entering a place that is special and has meaning beyond our ordinary lives.

Most of the other steps, from The Road of Trials to Master of Two Worlds can happen along the way as we train and progress. The Road of Trials is an obvious one! Who hasn't had trials in their lives, and that is especially true in aikido. One injury alone can be a nearly impossible trial to overcome. If you've traveled the aikido path for long enough, you have likely suffered an injury that made you question whether you could keep going.

The Master of Two Worlds is the place the hero goes after she has undergone the trials, has overcome temptation, and has gained the elixir (or boon) and returned the better person because of the success.

Each black belt test is a small version of the hero's journey. At the end, the tester has overcome the pain and exhaustion of intense practice, has overcome the temptations of quitting, and has gained the "boon," which is the rank itself. Each time we test we go on a little journey.

I'd like to think that at the end, the Freedom to Live, is

where the masters of the art live. Those teachers with the high ranks, the ones who teach and share their wisdom. The teachers who have been practicing the art for decades. They've overcome many of their temptations and left them behind. They've pushed through their trials and tests. That's all in the past. They've gained the elixir. Now what is left is to be Master of Two Worlds, the aikido world and the "real" world, and to have the Freedom to Live. This is the step where the hero is ready to live in the moment, afraid of neither life nor death.

Another aspect of the hero's journey that we experience in aikido is summed up in this quote by Campbell:

"You enter the forest
at the darkest point,
where there is no path.

Where there is a way or path,
it is someone else's path.

You are *not on your own path*.

If you follow someone else's way,
you are not going to realize
your potential." ~Joseph Campbell (italics added)

All of these steps, this entire journey, is something we have to do in our own way. In my essay *My Aikido Path*, I wrote about how I had visions that my reliance on my sempai was holding me back. It was my weakness to lean so heavily on them. While I underwent my "trial" of preparing for shodan, I understood I was "not on my own path," and I'd never realize my potential if I continued to use my sempai as a crutch. It was a hard lesson. But it was a good lesson.

We all have a path to follow whether we are practicing aikido or not. We are all on a hero's journey. It requires hard work and the discipline to show up day after day, but in the end, the elixir is within our grasp.

~2017

RESPONSIBILITY, TEACHING, TRAINING

☯

I wrote this for my sandan test in 2014. I was yet again in an entirely different place from when I tested for shodan and nidan.

Lining up to bow into class one afternoon, the teacher (a fellow yudansha) said, "Look to your left." We all looked to our left. "Those are all the people you are responsible for when training," she told us. Several people sat in seiza to my left.

"Now, look to your right." We all looked to our right. "Those are the people who are responsible for helping you." As the senior student that day, I turned to face a wall. No one was to my right.

In that moment I felt very alone. I felt the responsibility of what it means to be a senior student. Usually, during a night class when more yudansha are in attendance, I don't feel that weight of responsibility, but that afternoon it hit me. I am one of the senior students in this dojo, and I am responsible for a lot of people.

This kind of responsibility does not weigh lightly on me. Not at all. I take responsibility seriously, especially the responsibility of teaching others. When someone comes to a class I'm teaching, I want to be the best teacher I can be during that class and in that moment. I know I will never be perfect, and I will never be the right teacher for every student. I understand that some students will not like me or my teaching style. That's alright with me. But I never want anyone to say I wasn't prepared, I didn't know what I was doing, or I didn't care.

Because I care…a lot. As a senior student and as a teacher I care about the quality of my techniques and my ability. I watch other teachers and I see their unique habits and I think, "Which of my habits are students picking up on?" I think about my arched back, my lack of grounding, or even my odd hand movements. Will a student copy my peculiar flick of the wrist when I do certain techniques? I shudder to think that one of my cohai would mimic something specific to my own aikido, but I know it will happen from time to time. I've seen tests where I can clearly see which senior student the tester worked with during preparation. I've had people tell me they can see certain former sempai in my own techniques.

We all copy our teachers and sempai. That is why I feel the responsibility so heavily. That is why, right now, I am taking criticism of my own aikido more seriously than I have ever done before. As a senior student and sometime teacher, my aikido is no longer my own. It belongs to everyone. It is shared. That is a serious business.

Hoa Newens Sensei, in his book *Aikido Insights*, has an article about when you know you are ready to teach. The first step is when you feel a burning desire to teach. I can check that off my list. I love to share aikido with people and to help out my cohai. One of my struggles, though, is to not teach all the time. I have to regularly remind myself that when I'm training I'm not teaching. My training time is my time to practice and refine my own aikido. I can help my partner, but I'm starting to recognize that the best way to help my partner is to do good aikido, not talk them through everything. If my partner is a really new person, then a certain amount of verbal instruction is necessary. Aikido is really complicated when you are first starting, and we

Westerners are used to verbal instruction, so I tend to talk more when helping a brand new person. Unfortunately, I can get into the habit of talking with my peers as well. We have all given each other permission to critique and help when a technique is not working, and we take advantage of that. Even so, it's been my intention to guide my peers physically rather than verbally, by taking my partner's arm and moving it so he has my balance rather than telling him he doesn't have my balance.

Of course, this is still a work in progress. I still talk too much when practicing.

I also have the intention to not talk too much when I'm actually teaching a class. Here again, we don't need a lot of verbal instruction, especially if we are advanced. I want to be able to teach with my body, and not always with my mouth. One of the best compliments I ever received about my teaching was when a student who had only been practicing for a few months came up to me after class and told me she really liked my class, that I struck a good balance between talking and showing. I was pleased my efforts had paid off, but then the next time I taught I felt like a chatterbox! Like with aikido in general, my ability to teach aikido is a work in progress.

The Way of a Warrior
Cannot be encompassed
By words or in letters:
Grasp the essence
And move on toward realization!
~O'Sensei

Another thing Newens Sensei wrote in his book about teaching is this, "knowledge is a cumulative burden that needs to be continually unloaded unto others if the soul is to continue its travel." I think this relates back to saying you are ready to teach if you have a burning desire to share your knowledge. Perhaps the "burning desire" is the "burden" that needs to be released. I'm starting to wonder if the desire to teach, even inappropriately during training, is the need to unload our knowledge. We learn so much in aikido—physical, mental, emotional, and spiritual training builds up in our bodies and spirits. We only have so much "space" in ourselves to store all of this. After ten years of training, I think I've stored up quite a bit of aikido. Of course, it is a small amount compared to others who have thirty or forty years of training, but it's enough for my knowledge to start accumulating. It's like cramming a lot of stuff in a box. Only so much will fit; there is not infinite space. When it gets to the point where the lid to the box pops off, then it's time to get rid of some of what you've accumulated. Giving it away freely is the best way to free yourself of the stuff and help someone else in the process.

Back to responsibility. This is what I'm feeling so acutely at this point in my training—this desire to teach—this need to unload what I've learned. But I want to be sure what I'm teaching is right. I want to be sure my aikido is sound. Just because I have knowledge doesn't necessarily mean it's good knowledge. My focus is now on making sure my aikido is good enough to be up in front of a class teaching, because if I can't stand in front of a class and be confident I'm teaching aikido well, then I shouldn't be up in front of a class at all.

Perhaps that day when I looked to my right and saw no one standing next to me it was a message that I need to take care of myself as well as take care of those to my left. Now that I am a sempai and am teaching, I have to take care to continue to look after myself. The responsibility that rests heavily with me is a reminder to keep myself strong, continue to train and practice diligently, so I can pass on my knowledge and teach freely and confidently.

As O'Sensei said,
Day after day
Train your heart out,
Refining your technique:

Use the one to strike the Many!
That is the discipline of the Warrior.

~2014

DEFEATING EVIL WITH COMPASSION

I told a friend who practices aikido and likes *Lord of the Rings* that I like to write about both. A joke went around the table about Frodo doing aikido. I laughed but it got me thinking...Frodo does do aikido! As do two of my other favorite heroes. Here is how the aiki spirit of non-harming, of resolving conflict through love, plays out in three of my favorite stories.

How do we fight evil? With more force, bigger weapons, anger, hate?

What do our stories teach us? Let's look at my favorite three examples: *Harry Potter*, *Star Wars*, and *Lord of the Rings*.

In each story, there is a great evil pervading the land or universe. Great evil. Evil that wants to take over the entire world; evil that will stamp out all goodness. This is what the heroes in each of these stories are up against.

So how do Harry, Luke, Frodo and Aragorn defeat this kind of evil? With love, kindness, mercy, empathy, and compassion.

When Harry meets Voldemort at the end of the final book and they duel, Harry does not use the killing curse. He uses the simple expelliarmus spell, which only disarms an opponent. However, this creates a rebound effect on

Voldemort's killing curse.

The killing curse rebounds on Voldemort and kills him in turn. In essence, Voldemort's evil intent kills him. Harry does not kill Voldemort. He is merely the implement by which Voldemort's evil is destroyed.

At the end of *Return of the Jedi*, Luke fights and finally defeats Darth Vader...but he does not kill him. Luke cuts off Darth Vader's right hand, and in that moment, he recognizes himself in Vader. Luke looks at Vader's hand, looks at his own hand (which had been cut off by Vader), and recognizes he is becoming evil like Vader. He sees how his hate and anger will destroy him as it did Darth Vader. Luke deactivates his lightsaber as a sign of his disengagement with hate, anger, and evil. In the end, Darth Vader destroys the main force of evil in the galaxy, the Emperor. It is Luke's disengagement, his turning off the hate and anger—as symbolized by turning off his weapon— that propels the formerly evil Darth Vader to turn aside from his hate and anger and destroy the Emperor.

In *The Lord of the Rings*, Frodo shows mercy and compassion for Gollum all through the long journey towards Mordor to destroy Sauron's One Ring.

It is Frodo's mercy that eventually wins out in the end. When Frodo cannot destroy the evil, the One Ring, Gollum takes it from him and falls in the fire of Mt. Doom, thus destroying himself and the Ring. If Frodo had not shown empathy for Gollum (for, like Luke seeing himself in Darth Vader, he saw himself in Gollum) along the way, the Ring would not have been destroyed, and evil would have won.

Aragorn also does his bit. He is willing to sacrifice himself to give Frodo and Sam time to destroy the Ring. By storming the Black Gate of Mordor and distracting Sauron from seeing what was going on inside Mordor, he gives Frodo time. Aragorn believes he is doomed, he thinks he will die in that battle, but he is willing to do it all the same. His love for his hobbit friends makes him willing to sacrifice himself.

All four of these heroes do not only show that mercy, compassion, and love can defeat evil *in the end*. They show these traits *over and over again* throughout their journeys.

Every time Harry meets Voldemort (in whatever guise) he defeats him, not with evil, or some matched force, but with love or compassion. When they meet in the graveyard, Harry uses expelliarmus and this makes it so the specters of the people Voldemort killed appear out of Voldemort's wand. These specters all help Harry escape with his life. When Harry meets Voldemort in the Ministry of Magic and Voldemort tortures him, Harry does not turn to thoughts of vengeance; he thinks of his friends and family and how much he LOVES them. This overwhelming love breaks Voldemort's hold over him.

Luke shows compassion for Darth Vader when he is taken captive by Vader. He believes there is humanity and goodness in Vader if only he would let it out. Vader says it's too late for him, but Luke presses on. He never relents in his belief in Vader's inherent goodness, and this love and empathy save them all in the end.

Frodo, of course, shows mercy and compassion for Gollum the moment he sees him. At the beginning of his journey, he thought it was a shame that Bilbo hadn't killed him when he had the chance. But, once Frodo sees how much of a miserable creature Gollum is, Frodo can't help but pity him. He also shows empathy. He can see how he, too, could become like Gollum. He understands the terrible pull of the One Ring.

Fiction can teach us so much about life. These well-loved stories tell us that evil cannot be defeated and destroyed by anger, hate, stronger evil, or a better weapon. Evil is defeated by the even stronger human traits of kindness, compassion, mercy, and love.

As O'Sensei said,

"To injure an opponent is to injure yourself. To control aggression without inflicting injury is the Art of Peace."
~2014

RELEASE

Strength, confidence, power
Soft, kind, gentle.
It reaches inside my soul
The connection
Transforms me.

Darkness, anger, pain
leave my body.
A bubble
Burst in the light.

THE GIRL'S SHADOW: AN AIKIDO FABLE

☯

I woke up one morning with the following story in my head. I didn't know what to make of it, and I shared it with a couple of friends. One of my friends called it an "aikido fable." I like that term so I'm sticking with it.

Once, there was a girl who had a shadow. Of course, everyone has a shadow, but this girl's shadow followed her everywhere. She could see it in the house, and she could see it in the dark. Yes, even in the dark, it would follow her, standing up against the wall at night, all inky, like a black satin stain.

"Go away," she said.

"NO," the shadow answered, and it had a deep, deep voice like it had come up from the ground or out of the sky and had pulled in the whole world to say that one word.

The girl covered her head with her comforter and hid from the shadow, but she knew it was there. It was always there.

The girl asked her brother, "Can you see my shadow?"

Her brother sneered at her and thumped her on her forehead with his finger. "Dummy. You can't see a shadow inside the house." Smirking, he walked away.

The girls' shadow pulsed behind her.

Every night, the girl would say to the shadow. "Go away."

Every night, the shadow would say to the girl. "NO."

When the girl grew older, she wore all black to match her shadow.

Her mother said, "You'd look prettier if you wore this." She held up a flowery dress.

The girl turned away, her shadow heavy behind her.

One night, after the shadow refused to go away, the girl hid under her comforter like she always did, but this night she did not fall asleep. This night she grew angry. As she lay in her bed, she grew angrier and angrier until she flung back the covers, leaped out of bed, and threw herself at the shadow.

She hit it with her fists and kicked it and hit and kicked and hit and kicked, screaming at it.

"Go away! Go away!"

But the shadow did not go away. It grew stronger. With each punch and each kick, it grew stronger and harder until it felt like a cement wall.

A knock on the door and her mother's voice, concerned. "Are you alright?"

The girl, breathing hard, lying on the floor in the fetal position in front of her shadow as it loomed over her, called out. "Just a bad dream."

She listened as her mother went back to her room. She kicked out at the shadow one last time, but it did not move.

The next morning the girl woke on the floor of her bedroom, and before she opened her eyes she muttered to herself, it will be gone, it will be gone, it will be gone, like a mantra. When she opened her eyes, she gasped and let out a wailing moan.

The shadow had grown in the night. Taller. Thicker. Darker.

And she knew.

Fighting it had made it stronger.

The girl's alarm blared but she could not move to turn it off. Her nightstand felt so far away, much too far to get to, so it blared, beep, beep, beep, beep, until her brother banged on her bedroom door.

"Shut off your alarm!"

The girl roused herself off the carpet, keeping one eye on the shadow, and slapped her hand over the alarm, silencing it.

The girl went through her day with the shadow looming behind her. When she got home from school, she threw herself onto her bed, arms spread out, legs hanging over the edge, and stared at the ceiling. The shadow will not go away. If I fight it, it gets stronger. As she thought about it, the room grew dark, and she fell asleep.

She dreamed she was flying. Not flitting from rooftop to rooftop as she'd done in other dreams. No, this was really flying, arms spread out and zooming through the sky. She flew over her house, her street, her neighborhood, her town, out over mountains, forests, canyons, and the ocean. She flew and flew and flew.

She woke with a gasp. Turning her head slowly, she stared at the shadow. And stared. She rose slowly and stood in front of it. The shadow did not move.

"What are you?"

"I AM YOU."

She stepped back from the shadow. And she fled.

She ran out of her room, down the stairs, and out the front door. She ran and ran and ran until her breath came in ragged gasps and a stitch raced up her side like a knife had sliced through her. She stopped to catch her breath and looked back. The shadow was right behind her, as calm as the night.

And it had grown.

The girl sat down where she was, not caring that she was in a nearly empty parking lot, the lights illuminating the few remaining cars. She could hear the soft hum of the neon lights from the store sign.

She could not get rid of the shadow. She could not fight it. She could not outrun it. It would not go away.

With a resigned and weary sigh, she got up and headed

back home, the shadow right behind her. She went into her house and got into bed.

"Go away."

"NO."

The girl grew older and left her childhood home, but the shadow remained with her. She had stopped fighting it, but every night she still asked it to go away and every night it said no. She did not have friends or a partner because the shadow was too heavy, too much of a burden.

One night she had the flying dream again. She wanted to stay in the dream forever, to fly unfettered forever. When she woke, she bolted upright in her bed with a realization. In her dream, she had let the shadow go. That was how she could fly. She turned her head to look at the shadow. It was as it always was, standing against the wall of her room, silent, steady, oppressive.

The woman got out of bed and stood in front of the shadow. She recalled the night she had fought with it. This time she would not fight. Instead, she reached out her hand and placed her palm on the shadow. She hesitated at first, fearing what would happen, but nothing happened. It was warm to the touch, like touching someone who was asleep under the covers. She understood that she found comfort in the shadow, even as it weighed her down.

She took a deep breath and placed her other palm on the shadow. This time something happened. She could see and feel and hear a memory. Not one she wanted to remember, but one that needed remembering. As she felt it, the fear and anger melted away. It was so long ago, what was the point in hanging on to it?

Something hit the floor next to her foot. Drip. She looked down. A black drop hit the floor and then disappeared. Another drop, and then another, until a small puddle lay at her feet before disappearing into the floor.

She pulled her hands away from the shadow.

It had gotten smaller.

Tired, now, the woman climbed back into bed and fell

fast asleep.

The next night she dreamt of flying again and when she awoke again she placed her hands on the shadow until she could see and feel another memory. She let that one go. And another. And another until her room was a flood of black shadow slowly disappearing into the floor.

Every night the shadow grew smaller. Until one night.

The hardest memory. She clung to this one. What would she be without this memory? Would she even be herself? Would she disappear out of this world like the shadow, one drop at a time? The woman put her hands on the shadow and pulled them away as soon as the memory hit her. She could not do this. She went back to bed.

For many nights she tried to feel that last memory, to let it go, and for all those nights she failed. The shadow was small now, as small as the child she'd been when the memory happened. She was lighter and nearly free. But not quite.

One night, she rose, not tentative, not hesitating. She would do this tonight. As soon as she placed her hands on the shadow, she saw the memory, felt it, heard it, even smelled it. At first, she wanted to pull away again, but then she took a deep breath and dug her hands in even further. They sunk in, in, in, into the shadow, into the memory. Until…

The shadow burst into a million pieces. This time it did not drip drop onto the floor. This time it shattered like a sunburst, throwing the darkness everywhere before it dissipated like fog when the sun shines.

It was gone. The shadow was gone.

The woman lay on the floor and watched out the window as the sun slowly brightened the curtains, highlighting her room bit by bit. A ray of light landed on her calendar. It was the anniversary to the day of the event that happened to bring about the shadow. She had not known it. She got up off the floor, raised her hands above her head, and took a deep breath. It was light. Free.

She looked at the wall where the shadow had stood.
"Go away," she said.
There was no answer.

~2016

ACKNOWLEDGEMENTS

Thank you to everyone I have ever trained with in aikido. Aikido only works with partners, and I'm grateful to have worked with so many wonderful people.

Thank you to my teacher—Judith Robinson Sensei, 6th dan, who has been there for me every step of the way. When I walked into your dojo, I knew I'd come to the right place. You have nurtured my aiki spirit along with training my body. If it hadn't been for the respectful environment you cultivated in your dojo, I never would have walked this path.

Thank you to Hans Goto Shihan, 7th dan, my teacher's teacher who has taught at my dojo every year since I started in aikido. I will always be grateful to you for sharing your aikido with us and for sharing so many great stories!

Thank you to Mary Heiny Sensei, 7th dan, for all of your wonderful teachings and guidance along the way. Heiny Sensei is an inspiration to me and for all women in aikido.

I wish I could thank everyone personally, but I'm afraid I'll leave someone out! Thank you to my dojo mates, past and present, for all the times you've trained with me, guided me through a tricky technique, supported me through good and bad times, and threw me around until I was exhausted!

Thank you to my parents. Not everyone has parents who are so supportive. From second kyu on, you have been at every test, cheering me on. My mother loves to tell people that her tiny daughter is a third degree black belt.

My biggest thanks go to Blake and Hunter. I couldn't have asked for a more supportive husband and son. Thank you for being okay that I spent a lot of time at the dojo, for putting up with all the injuries, and for listening to me when I got all philosophical about my aikido journey. You've been there from the very beginning, and I know you will see me through to the end.

ABOUT THE AUTHOR

Kim Barton has been practicing Aikido for fifteen years under Judith Robinson Sensei, 6th dan, and holds the rank of 3rd dan from the Aikido World Headquarters in Japan.

You can read my blog or find out about my other books at my website:

www.ksbarton.com

Visit me on Facebook:
https://www.facebook.com/ksbartonauthor/

If you'd like to learn more about my dojo, Aikido at the Center in Tucson, AZ, please visit our website:

www.aikidoatthecenter.org